NIGERIA
the people

Anne Rosenberg

A Bobbie Kalman Book

The Lands, Peoples, and Cultures Series

Crabtree Publishing Company

www.crabtreebooks.com

The Lands, Peoples, and Cultures Series

Created by Bobbie Kalman

Coordinating editor
Ellen Rodger

Project development, photoresearch, and design
First Folio Resource Group, Inc.
  Erinn Banting
  Pauline Beggs
  Tom Dart
  Kathryn Lane
  Claire Milne
  Debbie Smith

Editing
Jessica Rudolph

Separations and film
Embassy Graphics

Printer
Worzalla Publishing Company

Consultants
Ibrahim Hamza, York University; Olatunji Ojo, York University

Photographs
AP/Wide World Photos: p. 29 (top); John Cole/Impact: title page, p. 15 (top); Corbis/Paul Almasy: p. 16 (both), p. 17 (top), p. 18 (right), p. 23 (bottom); Corbis/Bettman: p. 10; Corbis/Jerry Cooke: p. 30; Stephanie Dinkins/Photo Researchers: p. 6 (right); Christina Dodwell/The Hutchison Library: p. 15 (bottom); Werner Forman/Art Resource: p. 6 (left); p. 7 (both), p. 8 (left); Georg Gerster/Photo Researchers: p. 5 (bottom); Beryl Goldberg: p. 21 (left); Lori Hale: p. 20 (bottom), p. 24 (bottom), p. 31 (bottom); Juliet Highet/Hutchison Library: p. 3, p. 21 (right), p. 22 (right), p. 25 (bottom); The Hunger Project: p. 11 (bottom); Hutchison Library: p. 4 (bottom right), p. 12 (bottom), p. 14 (right), p. 20 (top), p. 29 (bottom); Jason Lauré: p. 13 (top), p. 29 (bottom); Giles Moberly/Impact: p. 5 (top), p. 13 (bottom); James Morris/Panos Pictures: p. 12 (top), p. 14 (left), p. 19 (both), p. 24 (top), p. 27 (bottom), p. 28 (top); North Wind Pictures: p. 8 (right), p. 9 (all); Photo Researchers: p. 4 (top right); Giacomo Pirozzi/Panos Pictures: cover, p. 17 (bottom), p. 22 (left), p. 23 (top), p. 26 (bottom); Betty Press/Panos Pictures: p. 4 (bottom left), p. 18 (left), p. 27 (top); Reditt/ Hutchinson Library: p. 21 (bottom); Reuters/Corrine Dufka/Archive Photos: p. 11 (top); Reuters/Grigory Dukor/Archive Photos: p. 28 (bottom); Candace Sharsu: p. 26 (top), p. 31 (top); Val & Alan Wilkinson/ Hutchinson Library: p. 25 (top)

Illustrations
Dianne Eastman: icon
David Wysotski, Allure Illustrations: back cover

Cover: A girl from Abuja, Nigeria's capital, wears a colorful dress and head-scarf.

Title page: A group of girls prepare for a day at the market in Ibadan.

Icon: A hut with a straw roof appears at the head of every section.

Back cover: Bush babies live in Nigeria's rainforests and savannas.

Published by
Crabtree Publishing Company

PMB 16A	612 Welland Avenue	73 Lime Walk
350 Fifth Avenue	St. Catharines	Headington
Suite 3308	Ontario, Canada	Oxford OX3 7AD
New York	L2M 5V6	United Kingdom
N.Y. 10118		

Cataloging in Publication Data
Rosenberg, Anne, 1964–
    Nigeria, the people / Anne Rosenberg.
      p. cm. -- (The lands, peoples, and cultures series)
    Includes index.
      ISBN 0-86505-248-4 (RLB) -- ISBN 0-86505-328-6 (pbk.)
      1. Nigeria--Social life and customs--Juvenile literature. 2. Ethnology--Nigeria--Juvenile literature. [1. Nigeria--Social life and customs.] I. Title. II. Series.

DT515.4 .R68 2000
966.9--dc21   00-043225
                                                                                          LC

Contents

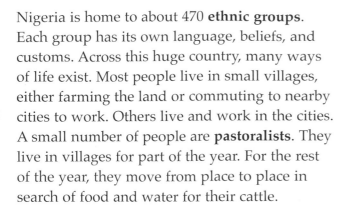

A home to many

Nigeria is home to about 470 **ethnic groups**. Each group has its own language, beliefs, and customs. Across this huge country, many ways of life exist. Most people live in small villages, either farming the land or commuting to nearby cities to work. Others live and work in the cities. A small number of people are **pastoralists**. They live in villages for part of the year. For the rest of the year, they move from place to place in search of food and water for their cattle.

Religious and political differences between Nigeria's peoples have led to many conflicts, including a **civil war** from 1967 to 1970. Today, Nigerians are working hard to bridge their differences and build a more united country.

Children get ready for recess at a school in Kaduna, in northern Nigeria.

This man of the Tuareg nomadic people, covers his head to protect himself from the hot sun.

A man bargains with a vendor at a market in Ibadan, in southeastern Nigeria.

Two girls, wearing head coverings and dresses made from colorful fabrics, stand in front of a store in Zaria, in northern Nigeria.

Families work together to empty their fishing nets. They will sell their fish at the local market.

Ancient peoples made this terracotta mask, which was discovered in Nok, around the seventh century B.C.

Nigeria has been an independent country only since 1960, but people have lived on the land for thousands of years. The earliest known inhabitants were the Nok. They lived in the north and central plains from about the seventh century B.C. to the third century A.D. **Archaeologists** first discovered evidence of this ancient civilization in the early 1940s when they uncovered **terracotta** sculptures in a tin mine near the northern town of Nok.

The Igbo also settled in the land thousands of years ago, making their homes in the forests of the southeast. Igbo communities were small. Each village was ruled by a council chosen from the most respected elders. People from nearby villages traded goods such as yams, palm oil, and **textiles** with one another.

Yoruba kingdoms

The Yoruba first came to what is now Western Nigeria around the first century B.C. Many more arrived between the ninth and thirteenth centuries A.D., led by a man named Oduduwa and his family. He and his children became the rulers, or **obas**, of the kingdoms of Ile-Ife, Oyo and Benin.

Many people believed that the *obas* were gods who neither ate nor slept. They lived in magnificent palaces filled with art that showed scenes of court life and stories from history. In Benin, majestic bronze masks and statues decorated the palace. In Ile-Ife, known throughout Africa as a center for art, even the streets were beautiful. They were decorated with elaborate designs made from pieces of broken pottery.

During the eleventh century, this statue of a powerful warrior stood in Ile-Ife.

A bronze plaque, with the head of a snarling leopard, decorated the palace of the oba of Benin.

Soldiers holding swords and shields guard the palace of the oba of Benin, on this plaque from the seventeenth century.

The Hausa and Fulani

The first Hausa settlements were established in the north between the eleventh and twelfth centuries. These early settlements were organized into seven kingdoms, called **city-states**, which were ruled by kings called *sarkis*. The city-states became important trading centers. They produced fine cloths and leather goods that attracted traders from all over North Africa. Kano and Rano, nicknamed "Chiefs of Indigo," were two city-states that became famous for their indigo, or blue cloth.

In the thirteenth century, another people, known as the Fulani, began to settle in the north. The leaders of the Fulani were religious chiefs called *emirs*. Each *emir* had an army and a royal court that included **merchants**, traders, musicians, doctors, and teachers.

Sarki the Snake

According to legend, the Hausa city-states trace their beginnings to a man named Bayajidda, a traveler from the Middle East. When Bayajidda journeyed to the Hausa town of Daura, he came upon Sarki, a powerful snake that only allowed people to take water from the town's well on Fridays. Wanting to free the people from Sarki's control, Bayajidda waited until night fell and used his sword to kill the monstrous snake. To thank Bayajidda for his heroic act, the queen of Daura, named Daurama, married him and bore him seven sons. Each son ruled over a Hausa city-state. From that day on, the Hausa called their kings *sarkis*.

The arrival of Europeans

In the late fifteenth century, Portuguese explorers arrived in the land, looking for places to trade their spices. They eventually built a trading post on the island of São Tomé, near the southern tip of present-day Nigeria. There, they exchanged their pepper for textiles with nearby village leaders. The trading post was so successful that traders soon began to come from Britain, France, and Holland.

During the seventeenth century, Europeans came to Nigeria in giant ships to explore and find riches.

A Portuguese explorer goes hunting with his dog on this sixteenth-century plaque from Benin.

Holy war

In 1804, a Fulani leader named Usuman dan Fodio started a holy war, or *jihad*, against the Hausa kings. Both the Hausa and the Fulani are Muslims. Muslims follow the religion of Islam. They believe in one God, whom they call Allah, and follow the teachings of his **prophet** Muhammad. Dan Fodio began the *jihad* because he believed that Hausa leaders did not follow the laws of Islam closely enough. His powerful armies swept through the city-states, and he encouraged people to rebel and to start *jihads* all over the north. Dan Fodio eventually conquered most of the area and replaced the Hausa kings with *emirs,* who governed the north according to the laws of the Qur'an, the Muslim holy book.

The slave trade

By the seventeenth century, European countries had established **colonies** in North, South, and Central America and in the islands of the Caribbean. They built huge farms, called plantations, in these new colonies where they grew sugar, cotton, coffee, and tobacco for European markets. To earn huge profits, plantation owners needed cheap labor. Slave traders rounded up people from Nigeria, herded them into forts on the coast, and shipped them out to work as slaves. Over ten million Africans were forced into slavery in far-off countries. There, they worked on plantations, earning no money and suffering under horrible conditions, until the slave trade was **abolished** in the mid-nineteenth century.

In this drawing from the 1800s, a group of Nigerians are being led to a slave ship.

Nigerian merchants lead their camels into the city of Kano in this drawing from the 1860s.

Colonizing Nigeria

In the late nineteenth century, the British ruled many countries throughout the world. It wanted Nigeria under its control, too. It especially wanted Nigeria's **natural resources**, which included gold, tin, and palm oil.

Britain sent its army to capture the land. Although local forces fought back, British troops were far more powerful. Over the next twelve years, they gradually acquired more land. In 1900, the British claimed Nigeria as a British colony.

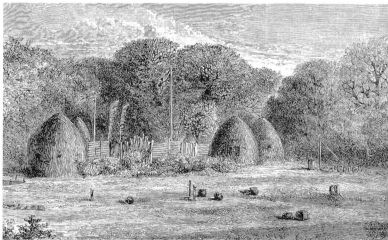

This drawing shows a British explorer's camp in 1870.

Fighting for independence

Nigerians were very opposed to British rule because they had no control over their own country. Their natural resources were sold in Europe and most of the profits went to Britain. Nigerians were forced to pay high taxes and were not allowed to vote. The British also treated some ethnic groups better than others. For example, they provided education for people in the south, but not for people in the north. Ethnic groups grew bitter and jealous of one another, especially the Igbo, who were educated and given government positions, and the Hausa, who were given neither education nor political power.

Nigerians grew more and more unhappy under British rule. They marched in protest and held strikes. The tension worsened and Nigerians put more pressure on Britain to grant them independence. Finally, on October 1, 1960, Britain agreed and the Federal Republic of Nigeria was born.

Crowds fill the streets of Lagos, in northern Nigeria, during a parade to celebrate the end of the Biafran War.

The Biafran War

A land of so many cultures and religions was difficult to unite. After independence, problems between ethnic groups continued. There was little agreement on who should control the land or even how regions should be divided. After two violent **coups** in 1966, the government changed the way each region was run. It gave new power to some people and took power away from others. The eastern part of the country was particularly unhappy with the change. Fighting broke out. The Igbo declared the eastern region, which they called Biafra, an independent country.

The Nigerian government wanted to keep Nigeria together and would not allow any group to break away to form its own country. It also wanted to support the non-Igbo people in Biafra who did not want to separate from Nigeria. Furthermore, the Nigerian government was afraid of losing profits from the sale of oil in Biafra.

Civil war began in 1967. The people of Biafra were cut off from food supplies, and hundreds of thousands died of starvation. The war ended in 1970, when the Igbo surrendered and the state of Biafra ceased to exist.

People cast their votes during a presidential election on February 27, 1999. This election ended fifteen years of military rule.

Chief Bisi Ogunleye

For nearly two decades, Yoruba chief Bisi Ogunleye has worked to free the women of Nigeria from hunger and poverty. In the beginning, she donated one month's salary to a group of rural women to start their own businesses. As these businesses became successful, the profits were used to start other businesses. Soon, women all over the country were starting their own businesses, working as shopkeepers and craftspeople. In 1982, Chief Bisi Ogunleye founded the Country Women's Association of Nigeria, an organization that works to improve the lives of women throughout the country. Today, the organization has grown from its original 150 members to a membership of over 31,000 people.

Nigeria today

For the past thirty years, Nigeria's government has been very unstable. The military has long ruled the country, with one group overthrowing another in violent coups. On May 29, 1999, military rule ended and a **democratic** government came to power. Although Nigerians still struggle with political and religious tensions, they have now elected a government that represents the whole population. Nigerians may at last be able to realize their dream of a more stable country.

People

A group of Yoruba women, dressed in colorful clothing, get ready to watch a parade in Benin City.

Long ago, Nigeria was a **crossroads** where traders from across Africa met. Over time, many different peoples settled on the land. Today, Nigeria has a population of 108 million people and is home to an enormous number of ethnic groups. The main groups are the Igbo, Yoruba, Hausa, and Fulani.

The Igbo

The Igbo live in the southeast part of Nigeria. They speak over thirty **dialects**, so Igbo from one village may not be able to understand Igbo from another. Family is very important to the Igbo. Parents encourage their children to remain in their villages to marry and raise their families. Most Igbo are Christians. Christianity is a religion based on the teachings of Jesus Christ, who is believed to be God's son on earth.

An Igbo man wears a traditional embroidered hat.

The Yoruba

The Yoruba live in busy cities in southwest Nigeria. Many **commute** from these cities to rural areas where they raise crops on small family farms. This is unlike most other Nigerians, who live in the country and commute to the cities for work. Many Yoruba are Christians, although some still observe traditional beliefs. *Obas* rule the Yoruba towns or villages, and are highly respected. The *obas* also advise the government about Yoruba traditions.

The Hausa

The Hausa make up the largest group of people in northern Nigeria. Most Hausa follow Islam and live according to *Shari'a* law, Muslim religious law. The city-states in which they once lived have become modern cities. Many are educational and business centers for the neighboring villages.

The Fulani

The Fulani live in the northern part of Nigeria. Some make their home in large cities. Others are pastoralists. In pastoral communities, the herders travel with their cattle during the dry season in search of good grazing land. During the rainy season, they live in villages where they grow grains such as **millet**, **sorghum**, and corn.

The pastoral Fulani know their cattle very well. The herders name all their cattle and sometimes even decorate them by painting their hides and heads with colorful blue dyes. They also teach their cattle to respond when called on the flute. The survival of the pastoral Fulani depends on their herds, since they make their living by selling milk and butter from their cows to villagers.

A Hausa man uses his donkey to carry home food and supplies.

Young Fulani women carry decorative bowls on their heads.

Village life

Over half of Nigeria's population lives in rural areas. Most of the people are farmers, who spend their days caring for their crops as their **ancestors** did.

A shared space
Almost every Nigerian village is organized into a compound. Within each compound is an enormous yard surrounded by houses. Whole families, including parents, children, aunts, uncles, and cousins, live there. Although each family has its own house, everyone shares the large yard and garden.

Time for chores
In villages, the day starts before sunrise. Men head out to work in the fields, plowing and planting crops. Women take care of the children, look after the house, tend to the family vegetable plot, and prepare meals. In the afternoon, when school is over for the day, children help by feeding the farm animals and collecting water for cooking and bathing. Boys also gather firewood and learn how to plant crops, while girls do light housework such as sweeping the floor or putting water on the fire for the evening meal.

A woman pounds cassava, a root vegetable used in many Nigerian dishes.

Family ties
Parents, children, aunts, uncles, grandparents, and cousins are all part of the extended family in Nigeria's villages. If someone's crop fails, family members share their food. If a house needs to be repaired, relatives lend a hand.

Nigerian families also spend time together in the evening, after the hard work of running a farm is done. They gather to tell tales from ancient times and stories about their village's past and present. In this way, they pass on their culture from generation to generation.

Hardships
Life in the countryside can be very difficult. Much of the country's farmland has been damaged by long periods of drought, or lack of water. Many men are forced to look for work outside their villages. Some travel for hours each day to work in the cities, while others move to the cities permanently, sending money to support the families they leave behind.

A grandfather and his two grandsons take a break from their daily chores.

14

A farmer herds his cattle into a clearing to graze on shrubs and bushes.

Homes and buildings where food and grain are stored are built into the side of a hill on the Jos Plateau, in northern Nigeria.

🛖 City life 🛖

Many of Nigeria's cities are a blend of old and new. Ancient palaces and **mosques** dating back to the fourteenth century stand alongside gleaming skyscrapers and fast food restaurants. These cities have become much larger over the past few decades as businesses and industry have grown and as people have come looking for work.

A bustling scene

Nigerian cities are busy places. Each day, millions of people travel from rural areas to their jobs in the cities. Many work in factories or office buildings. Others are teachers, **engineers**, or doctors.

When noon arrives, the city hums with life as people run errands, chat with friends, and lunch on the country's most popular fast-food, *suya*. *Suya* is spicy beef or goat meat served on a stick. After work, most people cram into cars and buses for the commute home. Others stay downtown to have dinner at a restaurant or to enjoy a movie or play.

(above) Homes with tin roofs crowd the streets of Ibadan.

(top) Two young women chat while shading themselves from the sun with an umbrella.

16

So much traffic!

Nigerian cities are famous for their traffic jams. During rush hour, the streets are packed with cars, buses, trucks, and bicycles. These traffic jams are a main source of income for thousands of Nigerians who work as street vendors. They weave through the stopped vehicles, selling drinks, nuts, sweets, watches, and makeup to frustrated drivers.

Overcrowding

With so many people moving from the villages to the cities in search of work, Nigeria's cities have become overcrowded. There is not enough proper housing for everyone, so the very poor live in **shantytowns** on the outskirts of the cities. They build houses out of mud, iron sheets, plywood, or any bits of metal or cardboard that they can find. There is no electricity, running water, or garbage pickup in the shantytowns, so trash piles up everywhere.

Even within the cities, basic services such as electricity and water are unreliable. Power outages are a routine part of the day, and people often do not have enough water for their daily needs.

A vendor stands on the roof of a bus, selling snacks to people who are boarding the bus.

Traffic slows to a standstill in Lagos.

A variety of homes

People build their homes to suit their **environment**. In the north, where it is hot and dry, clay or mud houses provide shelter from the scorching sun. In the wet climate of the south, **bamboo** is used to keep out the heavy rains.

City houses

In the city, most people live in one-story homes with a small kitchen, bathroom, living room, and one or two bedrooms. In older neighborhoods, many houses are in poor condition and are crowded together without any yards. In the wealthier neighborhoods, the houses are much larger. Some have a courtyard where families can sit and talk on a warm night.

Houses, apartment buildings, and businesses stand beside one another in a neighborhood in Lagos.

Country homes

People who live in the countryside use mud or clay to build the walls of their houses and tin or woven grasses to make the roofs. These materials help keep out the sun's heat. Most houses are simple one-room homes with a dirt floor and no running water or electricity. The doorstep is often high above the ground so snakes cannot slither inside. Meals are prepared around a stone fireplace in the middle of the house. Although families may have a stool or chair for visitors, they eat and sleep on woven mats on the floor. Homes in the country all share the same basic style, but the houses of each ethnic group have their own special features.

A family gathers outside their apartment building.

Homes of the Hausa

Hausa who live in the countryside have round houses made of clay, with **thatched** roofs that rise to a cone shape. Their homes have such tiny doors that people have to duck to go in and out. Hausa who live in cities have much larger homes. They are square-shaped and made of cement or stone, with flat roofs. In very hot weather, people even sleep on the roof!

Children play outside while their brother helps make dinner under the grass roof of their home.

A house on the Jos Plateau is supported by elaborately carved pieces of wood and is covered by a thatched roof.

Sloping roofs

Yoruba houses in the countryside are made of mud bricks, with wooden doors and window frames. The roofs, which are usually made of iron, slope downward. During the wet season, people place buckets by the side of their house to collect rainwater as it runs down the roof. When the hot weather comes, the overhanging roofs provide shelter from the afternoon sun.

Waterproof houses

The Igbo live in the rainy areas of southeast Nigeria, so their houses need to be waterproof. Igbo homes have no windows. The walls are made from bamboo poles tied with vines and sealed with clay, and the roofs are made from banana leaves. Bamboo and banana leaves do not absorb moisture, so they help keep the rain out.

Laundry hangs on the front porch of a house in Oshogbo, in western Nigeria.

A town with houses made from mud bricks and iron roofs sits on the edge of the Niger River Delta, in southern Nigeria.

On stilts

In the swampy regions of southern Nigeria, people live in houses made from mangrove trees. Mangrove trees do not rot when they get wet. The homes are built on stilts high above the water, so they are protected from flooding caused by tropical rains. During the rainy season, people canoe right up to their home, then climb wooden stairs or a ladder to get inside. During the dry season, when the rivers are dry, people seek shelter from the hot African sun in the cool shadows under their houses.

A café in Warri, in southwestern Nigeria, is built on stilts like many of the homes in the area.

Fulani homes

The Fulani live in different types of homes, depending on how and where they live. Fulani in cities live in one-story houses. Pastoral Fulani make temporary homes by tying poles or branches together and covering them with tightly woven straw or grasses. These homes are easy to fold and light enough for their cattle to carry. In villages, where the herders live during the rainy season, they build round huts made of mud, with roofs that are made of thatch. During the dry season, the roofs are opened at the top, creating a small hole that allows heat and smoke from cooking to escape. During the rainy season, the hole is closed up again to keep the rain out.

Old clay homes still stand in Cikin Birni, the ancient part of Kano, in central Nigeria.

Nigerians eat many different kinds of food, depending on where they live. Main foods of the Yoruba, who live in the rainy southwest, are **yams** and **cassavas**. Cassavas are root vegetables that are shaped like carrots, with brown skin and white, starchy flesh. The Igbo eat fresh fish and citrus fruit, which are common in the wet climate of the southeast. For the Hausa, grains such as millet and sorghum, which grow in the north, are a main part of every meal. The Fulani cattle herders of northern Nigeria enjoy fresh milk and butter. *Suya* is a favorite snack everywhere.

Mealtime

Nigerian meals usually involve one main dish. Breakfast might be a thick porridge made from pounded grains. Lunch might consist of dried ground beans, which are eaten with a corn paste. For supper, many people eat dumplings made from ground millet and served with a spicy onion-and-tomato sauce.

A mother stirs a pot full of sauce, while her children await their dinner.

Spicy delights

Soups and stews, which are usually fiery hot, are a part of most meals. They take many hours to cook. A favorite Yoruba dish is *egusi*, a thick stew made with meat, hot chilies, bits of crushed cassava leaves, and ground seafood such as prawns. Another Yoruba favorite is *obe ata*, or fish and pepper soup, which is usually served with pounded yams for a filling supper.

Girls peel the thick brown skin off cassavas which have been grown on their families' farms.

Two girls make dumplings, which they will sell to hungry shoppers at the market.

Delicious drinks and desserts

To quench their thirst, Nigerians drink the tasty juice of the kola nut, which grows on kola trees in the southwest. For dessert, they often eat sweet, fried pastries, or fruit, such as mangos and pineapples, dipped in honey.

A favorite treat is baked or boiled **plantain**, a type of banana found in Nigeria, with cream poured on top. Try making it with an adult's help.

You need:
- one ripe but firm plantain or banana
- 1 tsp. (5 ml) lemon juice
- 1 tbsp. (15 ml) brown sugar
- 1/4 cup (60 ml) cream
- one handful crushed peanuts (optional)

Place the bananas in a pan with their skins on. Cook them in the oven at 350° Fahrenheit (180° Celsius) for twenty minutes. When the bananas cool down, peel them and sprinkle on lemon juice and brown sugar. Pour on cream and add crushed peanuts if you wish.

A man at a market in Kano cooks skewers of meat in the sand around a fire-pit.

 # To market

In Nigeria, each large village has an outdoor market. People shop here, visit friends, catch up on the day's news, and listen to musicians play *kalengo* drums.

A vibrant, noisy place

Nigeria's markets are a feast of colors and aromas. Hundreds of vendors sell fresh vegetables and spices. The smells of dried fish and roasted corn fill the air. If people need a snack, they can buy fried yam chips or *suya*. Vendors who sell the same types of goods sit together in long rows of stalls. As shoppers wander down these rows, they may discover items such as woven cloths, delicate glass beads, gold and silver jewelry, or leatherwork. Some vendors in larger markets even sell televisions, cars, and camels!

(right) Two merchants display vibrantly colored cloth at their stall in the busy Iddo market in Lagos.

(bottom) Shoppers bargain with vendors before purchasing goods at market.

To market, to market

Some vendors drive their goods to the market in brightly painted trucks. They stop at villages along the way to pick up customers and other vendors. By the time they reach the market, their trucks are jammed with people and goods! Other vendors bring their supplies to market on foot, carrying their goods in huge baskets on their heads.

Bargaining

There are few set prices in a market, so people bargain for goods. The buyer offers one price, the seller suggests a higher price, and so on until they agree. Not all goods can be bargained for, however. When people try to negotiate the prices of gold and silver, vendors are insulted. These prices are fixed.

Goats tied to fences wait to be inspected by farmers at a livestock market.

Some markets sell just one type of good. This market in Oshogbo specializes in containers such as bottles, jugs, and jars.

25

School days

Until recently, education in Nigeria was expensive. Many children whose families could not afford to send them to school never learned to read and write. When the government introduced free elementary education, more children were able to go to school and have a chance at a better life.

Early years
Children in Nigeria start school when they are six years old. Classes begin at 8:00 a.m. Children study reading, writing, science, and math, and are expected to work hard. Not all learning takes place in a classroom. Some schools have farming programs where students learn how to cut grass, hoe farmland, and plant vegetables and flowers.

Most schools have an assembly every morning. During the assembly, one student reads a prayer, another reads a poem, and another reads the school announcements. In the middle of the morning is a break for recess. Students play soccer and other games, such as The Big Snake, which is the Nigerian version of tag. After school, many students take part in team sports such as soccer and basketball.

(top) Children in bright blue and yellow uniforms wait in line for school to begin.

School clothes
In Nigerian schools, neatness is very important. Most girls have short or braided hair. Boys are not allowed to have long hair or to wear jewelry. Many schools design their own uniforms which the students must wear every day. The only time the students can wear their regular clothes at school is at parties or sports events. At other times, if they do not wear their uniforms, their teachers may send them home.

A girl copies down the notes that her teacher writes on the chalkboard.

Muslim children study parts of the Qur'an, written on large tablets, at a school in the countryside.

Three young women graduate from Benin University.

Special schools

Muslim children go to special religious schools where they study the Qur'an and become familiar with *Shari'a* law. A religious teacher, or *mallami*, teaches the students to read and write in Arabic, the language in which the Qur'an is written. When they have learned enough Arabic, the children must memorize long verses of the Qur'an.

The children of Fulani herders have traveling schools. Often, a teacher moves with the people and gives the day's lessons under a tree or in a field, wherever the children happen to be.

Few supplies

There are millions of school children in Nigeria but not enough schools or teachers to educate them. Sometimes, there are so many pupils that three or four students share one desk. The schools do not have enough money to provide pens or pencils to everyone, so students who can afford to, bring their own.

Higher education

After elementary school, students who wish to go to high school must pass an exam. There are many students and not enough schools, so there is a great deal of competition. After high school, some students go to university or vocational school, where they learn trades such as nursing or agriculture.

Sports and leisure

For centuries, people in Nigeria have held wrestling matches, archery competitions, and rowing or swimming meets. Today, sports and games are still favorite pastimes. Soccer, basketball, field hockey, cricket, boxing, and rugby are all played in clubs throughout the country, while horse racing and table tennis are popular in the north.

Soccer

Soccer, or "football" as Nigerians call it, is the country's most popular sport. Whenever a team is playing, fans pack the stadium, cheering for their favorite players. In 1996, Nigeria became the first African country to win the Olympic gold medal in soccer. After the winning goal, Nigerians raced through the streets, shouting and cheering with joy. Overhead, the skies lit up with firecrackers, and the country became a sea of green and white as people everywhere flew the Nigerian flag.

At play

Soccer is not just a spectator sport in Nigeria. Many people enjoy a relaxing game after a hard day's work. They play in parks and playgrounds, in fields or streets — wherever they can find an open space. If they do not have a soccer ball, they make one by tying a bunch of old rags together.

People watch a group of friends play a game of cards.

A soccer player jumps sideways in the air to reach the ball. Soccer is Nigeria's favorite sport.

Jumping the beanbag

Jumping the beanbag is one of Nigeria's most popular children's games. You can play it with some friends! Form a large circle around one player. The person standing in the center, the "swinger," holds a rope with a beanbag tied to one end. He or she swings the rope close to the ground. The other players must jump over the rope when it reaches them. If the rope hits a player, that player is out of the game. The last person left wins.

Film and TV

Going to the movies is another favorite pastime. In the evenings, many people who live in cities head to outdoor theaters, where they watch movies from Nigeria, China, the United States, and various European countries. Televisions are still uncommon in rural areas because few people have electricity. However, some villages now have large public viewing areas with television sets where people gather to enjoy a show or two.

A young boy gets ready for a ride on the Ferris wheel at a beach in Lagos. This Ferris wheel was made by hand. It is also turned by hand.

National Sports Festival

Since 1973, Nigeria has held the National Sports Festival every two years. This festival is held to discover young, talented athletes in all types of sports. Participants come from all over the country to compete in track-and-field, swimming, gymnastics, and many other athletic events. The most promising athletes are invited to amateur training camps to receive private coaching. Later, they compete at international tournaments.

Riders get ready for a horse race in Jos, in central Nigeria.

"Aina, time to get up. Wake up, or you'll be late for school!" Aina can hear the bang and clank of pots as her mother makes breakfast. Slowly, she opens her eyes.

"Aina? Come and eat your breakfast before it gets cold." It is only 6:30 a.m., and the air is chilly. Aina wraps her shawl around her and goes to wash her face in the little wooden basin. She slips on her school uniform, a white blouse and blue smock.

Aina's mother is standing at the fireplace, stirring porridge, or *asaro,* in the big clay pot. She carefully spoons the *asaro* into bowls for Aina and her sister, Nafisa. Aina quickly eats her breakfast, rolls up her sleeping mat, and gathers her books for school. "O dàbò," she says, giving her mother a quick hug goodbye. "Don't forget," Nafisa calls out. "Father promised us stories tonight." "I won't forget. Don't worry!" Aina is excited. After supper, Aina and Nafisa will sit in the courtyard, listening to tales of ancient kings and heroes. She wonders if her father will tell them again about *Emir* Mousa, who was so wealthy that he needed 1,000 camels to carry his gold!

"Aina!" her best friend, Monisola, calls as she steps outside. Aina and Monisola walk to and from school together every day. At 8:00 a.m., the bell rings. Aina's favorite subject, history, is first. After that, it is time for the school assembly. Aina reads the announcements, her voice trembling just a little. There is still agriculture class before lunch, but learning to take care of crops is hard work and her stomach is growling.

Aina tries hard to pay attention to her teacher. She can't wait to go home to hear her father's stories.

Finally, the bell rings. Aina and Monisola go and sit in the long grasses behind the school, where they eat their plantain and yam chips. After lunch, they join their classmates in a ball game. Climbing onto each other's backs, the children form a circle, throwing the ball from one pair to the next. "Throw it to me!" they call.

At 3:00 p.m., school is finished. Aina and Monisola pick pineapples on the way home, shaking the tree's branches to collect the sweet fruit. Thump! They have to duck to avoid the fruit. Thump! Thump!

At home, Aina helps her mother sweep and prepare supper, stirring the heavy pot of *egusi* over red-hot coals. Aina loves this stew, with its spicy meat and hot chilies. After dinner and homework, her father calls. "Aina and Nafisa, if you're done, come and listen to a story — or are you too tired?" "No, never!"

Aina's father doesn't tell about *Emir* Mousa. Instead, he tells a wonderful tale about the powerful *Oba* Ewuare of Benin, who protected his palace by building a wall around it and burying a magic charm under each of the wall's gates. Afterward, Aina and Nafisa roll out their sleeping mats for bed. "Do you think the story's true?" Aina whispers. "I don't know," says Nafisa. "It could be." Outside, the cisticola bird sings its sweet song. But the girls don't hear. They are already asleep.

On their way home from school, Aina and Monisola see a man selling onions at the market.

Aina's family and neighbors gather outside her home.

Glossary

abolish To cancel or do away with

ancestor A person from whom one is descended

archaeologist A person who studies the past by looking at buildings and artifacts

bamboo A woody plant with hollow stems

cassava A starchy root vegetable that is shaped like a carrot

city-state An independent state made up of a city and the area around it

civil war A war between different groups of people or areas within a country

colony An area controlled by a distant country

commute To travel from one place to another, usually for work

coup The overthrow of a government

crossroads A place that is centrally located

democratic Elected by the people

dialect A version of a language

emir A Muslim king or religious leader

engineer A person who uses science to design and build structures and machines

environment The conditions where one lives

ethnic group A group of people who share a common race, language, heritage, or religion

merchant A person who buys and sells goods

millet A type of grain used in cereals

mosque A Muslim place of worship

natural resource A material found in nature such as oil, coal, minerals, or lumber

oba A king

pastoralist Leading the life of a shepherd or herder

plantain A tropical fruit resembling a banana

prophet A person who is believed to speak on behalf of a god

shantytown A poor area in or outside a city where most people live in run-down homes

sorghum A type of grain used to make syrup

suya Spicy meat served on a stick

terracotta A hard, waterproof ceramic clay of brownish-orange color used to make pottery

textile A fabric or cloth

thatched Made of straw, reeds, or palm leaves woven together

yam A type of sweet potato

Index

1 2 3 4 5 6 7 8 9 0 Printed in the USA 5 4 3 2 1 0 9 8 7 6

9/ 0 6, 9